Life Goes On

Johnny Hart

CORONET BOOKS
Hodder and Stoughton

Copyright © 1978 by Field Enterprises, Inc.

First published in the United States of America
by Ballantine Books in 1984

Coronet edition 1986

British Library C.I.P.

Hart, Johnny
   Life goes on.
   I. Title
   813'.54[F]   PS3558.A68/

   ISBN 0-340-39340-8

Printed and bound in Great Britain for
Hodder and Stoughton Paperbacks, a
division of Hodder and Stoughton Ltd.,
Mill Road, Dunton Green, Sevenoaks,
Kent (Editorial Office: 47 Bedford
Square, London, WC1 3DP) by
Hunt Barnard Printing Ltd.,
Aylesbury, Bucks.

feck·less *adj*

ineffecktual

14

aah´

what a person's vocabulary is reduced to,

when you hold down their tongue with a stick.

interloper *n.*

an obnoxious relative that arrives by mail

sit·com

17

a new name for situation comedy,

which has been crying for a new name.

hart

1·10

112

LOOK, LOOK,
SEE DICK
SMILE.

1·7

OH, LOOK,
SEE JANE
SMILE.

DICK AND
JANE ARE
PLEASED.

SPOT HAS DONE A
CRITIQUE ON THE
NEWS MEDIA.

1·23

2.1

29

2·23

2·25

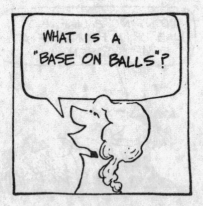

31

3.4

3.6

MISH·MASH

What a guy does when he gets drunk and doesn't wake up for church.

3·7

3.14

THE TOWN I LIVED IN,...

WAS SO SMALL,...

3·25

THE COURTHOUSE ONLY HELD ONE PIGEON.

YOU CANT FIGHT CITY HALL

3·29

3-30

4-3

45

4.6

4-21

4-27

4-28

5.1

5·15

516

5-23

5.25

26

KRACKLE
CRUNCH
SPLINTER
SPLINTER
SPPORK

5-27

5.30

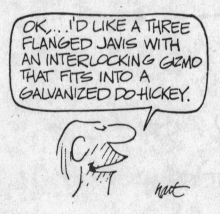

WELL, JOHN, IT'S OFFICIAL. THEY'VE CANCELLED THE ELECTION.
WHAT FOR?
11·6
I GUESS THEY'VE "HAD IT" WITH THE GOVERNMENTAL JUNK.
TOO BAD, IN A WAY, ...NO MORE DEALING, NO MORE KICK-BACKS, NO MORE FAVORS, NO MORE BACK-BITING, NO MORE COVER-UPS, NO MORE SCANDALS .....
LIFE GOES ON
hart

About the Author

As far back as he can remember, Johnny Hart has been drawing funny pictures, which have gotten him into or out of trouble, depending on the circumstances. It wasn't until he was nineteen and met young cartoonist Brant Parker, however, that he seriously began to consider cartooning as a profession. In the years that followed, that ambition grew—nurtured by Hart's wife, Bobby, who stood by him as he labored over kitchen tables far into the night, hoping to join the fraternity of cartoonists he idolized.

In 1959, his dream came true when B.C. ran nationally for the first time. THE WIZARD OF ID followed five years later, co-created by Brant Parker. Hart has gone on to win many major awards for his cartoons, including the prestigious Reuben Award for Cartoonist of the Year, in 1968. He and his wife live in upstate New York.

An interesting sidelight to this whole saga, Hart tells us, is that many of the characters in his strips are patterned after true, real-life friends.

That wasn't too smart.